I.C.U

LOVE ON THE LINE

PAVAN SAI CHANDRA
MUNNANGI

Contents

Dedication & Thank You

Dear Mom and Dad

Thank you for always being there for me and for your encouragement.
You both have made numerous sacrifices and taught me to never give up, to always smile, and to confront even the most difficult situations.

This one's for you both <3

Thank you Afsha Azmath ji (Author of "Life of a Twenster") for your unwavering support and wisdom along this journey. You were and always will be my mentor and your unflinching faith in me was inspiring.

Thank you, God, for this chance to shine.
and Finally my dear Sisters and brother-in-laws,

my friends VK, CN, DR, KN, MM.

Thank you all for your love and support.

Prologue

Dec 11, 2019

My phone started ringing. As I looked at it, it showed a landline number from a hospital. Thanks for the truecaller era. I didn't think it was important, but I decided to respond anyway. I recognised a familiar voice, and it was her friend Archana. She was sobbing so hard I could hardly make out anything that she was blabbering. In between the broken sobs she gave me the name of the hospital and asked me to reach there ASAP. Nothing made any sense to me. I asked her what was wrong. In one breath she uttered "Aadhya,".
My world spinned so fast, I couldn't understand anything but her name turned my eyes moist and my heart beat paced. I was filled with a million thoughts, I wasn't aware till I heard my own sound vibrating through the room "What happened to her?" Is she alright?

Please come to this hospital right away in KPHB, she said.

I told my parents I had to leave and would be late and dashed out the door, forgetting to take the bike keys. I went back to fetch the keys and fell down the stairs, bruising myself on the way, but I didn't really care as she was the only one on my mind at that moment.

Despite being just a 2-kilometer drive, it appeared to take forever. When I got to the hospital, I asked the receptionist for the room number.

I.C.U., she said.

"I.C.U," I hollered.

I was at a loss for words. I sprinted like a lunatic, my eyes searching for that one person who holds my heart.

As soon as I arrived at the I.C.U. ward, my lips began to quiver and started a silent prayer on their own. I saw Aadhya's mom, dad, and her brother standing and crying, watching someone in the intensive care unit. I saw my friends along with hers. I stood there dumbstruck, unable to move when someone grabbed my wrist. It was Ayaan, her brother. He had pleaded with me to go inside and talk to Aadhya.

Aadhya was in the I.C.U. with all the wires attached, I could see her heartbeat on the screen, yet my eyes refused to believe what they saw. I can't even feel the ground beneath me. My feet were numb and my palms ice cold. My world had already crumbled with that one phone call.

I was startled to hear when a voice ask, "Are you Mr. Abhiram?"

With tears in my eyes, I said yes to the nurse while my eyes still glued to Aadhya.

Please don't take too long, she needs to rest. The nurse exited the room, leaving the two of us alone.

I sat beside her bed, taking her hand in mine. She was

lying still surrounded by all the tubes and wires yet nothing could take away the beauty that she held. Even in that stillness, she was the most beautiful, most precious person to me on this earth.

I knew she couldn't hear me but I had to try.

I went near her ear and whispered softly.*Aadhya..

"Abhi....," echoed a voice.

CHAPTER I

When I first saw her

Jul 9, 2019

I can still recall the date. The time was 7:00 PM on July 9, 2019. Everyone in India was glued to the television for India's World Cup semi-final match against New Zealand. But I was with my father in the hospital for a routine checkup. I checked with the nurse only to discover that there are 15 people ahead of us waiting to see the doctor. It was 7:17 PM and I was no longer in mood, so I stopped checking the score, hoping that Dhoni would finish it off in style, but I received a message saying my favorite player was out. Disappointment washed over me and I was devastated to hear that India had lost the match. My day was heading nowhere good.

Around 7:30, I was almost blinded by a sparkling light only to realize it was a girl smiling from across the hall. She was dressed in a black top and blue jeans, with a lovely smile, and long dark hair which she wore loose. They were falling on her face, so she adjusted it partially revealing her face. It all happened in slow motion, and there it hit me that it happens not only in movies, but also in real life, but only with the right person.

As I looked at her, she walked towards me.

With my dad beside me, I was shit scared and thought I was going to die, but she reached for a glass of water from the desk beside me and walked past me. I could literally feel the freshness she brought with her. Suddenly, the hospital transformed into a paradise. I couldn't smell Dettol or hear people's voices anymore, all I could smell were flowers and look at her smile and the echo of her footsteps.

She then gestured to her mother, who was standing in the corner of the hall, and made her sit across from us. My heart pounded so hard. While my soul was content with her presence, my mind was pleading with me to ask her name, but I already anticipated the next scenario, so I was enjoying the beautiful atmosphere she had created and taking everything good that comes along with it.

My father's name was announced by the nurse, but I didn't hear because I was lost in my own train of thoughts. Out of nowhere, she began waving at me. I panicked, only to realize that it was my father's turn to see the doctor. I walked inside still dumbfounded by her smile. I was nowhere in the moment and only thought about her and her smile while the Doctor was giving me the instructions of what to do next. I returned to see her, but she was nowhere to be seen. My eyes scanned the hall but on not finding her around I thought to myself that I might not see her again. The feelings were let down by my heart but somehow I liked it because I had never felt that way about any girl before. It felt like the movies- the love of my life. With a disappointed face, I returned home with my father, reliving every single moment of what happened in the hospital.

We had an appointment scheduled after the next 5 days and I had to take my father for his routine check. And voila, it's the same one where I saw her. The saint and devil in me prayed for the girl to be there as well with her mother, like the last time. I felt so childish praying for someone to be in the hospital but it's what my heart desired in that moment..

While I waited patiently in the waiting area, my prayers were answered. She was sitting two rows ahead of us, dressed in a yellow white churidar with a bindi on her forehead and kohl clad eyes but this time without a smile, She kept whispering in her mother's ears, maybe consoling her about something.

We sat behind her and even though she couldn't see me, all I could see was her! The Nurse shouted in her hoarse voice "Aadhya".

It's me, she said slowly standing up.

Aadhya!. Aadhya..!

Her name was as lovely as she herself. But it even confused me a bit as to why her name is on the patient's list, and if I was calculating right, in this case, Aadhya was the patient.

I was nervous.

Is she alright? What happened to her? She is so young. I had so many questions and I didn't even know that person, but I was praying for her well-being. And just to put my mind at ease, the nurse said, "Please take your mother inside."
Relief flooded over me like a water splash. I said a silent prayer and smiled to myself.
They entered, and we were asked to meet the doctor in his office.

I didn't see her when we got out and assumed they'd gone. But my eyes were still looking for her when I heard a voice calling my name. I turned around to see her standing by the medical shop. She caught me staring at her, and I quickly turned away. I turned slowly again, but she was already looking at me.

I panicked because I didn't know what would happen next and quickly told my father that we needed to go home.

And I heard a sweet voice calling out my name as we were about to leave the hospital.

Abhiram!

I slowly turned around to face her, shocked and worried, not knowing what to expect as she unexpectantly handed me my debit card, which I had forgotten at the medical shop. She handed it to me with a smile, and I took it as if it were her personalized gift.

I was so happy because we knew each other's names, but how to start a conversation was still the biggest question for me.

And then it dawned on me that my father was waiting in the parking lot for a while now and I rushed back to him. When we finally arrived home, all I could think about was her sparkling eyes and beautiful smile. I had never liked my name so much until she said it.

Abhiram!!!

CHAPTER II

Visiting her house

Aug 5, 2019

I kept picturing her, her smile, and her face every day. Is this attraction or Love? I continued thinking about it since I had never felt that way before.
Surprisingly, the hospital has become my favourite spot, and all of the sounds, Dettol scent, and other distractions have fled, leaving just fresh air and a lovely perfume. Is this how falling in love feels like?
It felt so silly.
Going to the hospital after work has become a daily habit.

And, as usual I went to the hospital to pick up my father's reports, while I was leaving, I heard a voice.

Beta! Beta!

I turned to see if it was for me, and to my shock it was Aadhya's mother.

Yes, Aunty.

Son, My phone's battery died. Can I use your phone to make a call?

Sure thing, aunty. I handed her my phone and hoped she would call Aadhya.

She spoke with someone and handed me the phone, saying, Thank you beta.

It's fine, Aunty. Is anyone coming to pick you up?

Ha beta, I came here to get my reports, and my daughter should have come by now, but she didn't, and my phone battery died, so I'll have to wait another hour.

Okay.
.

.

.

Where do you stay Aunty?

Near KPHB Metro station

Oh!

Aunty, If you don't mind, I'll drop you off at home.

No son, it's okay, I will wait.

It won't be an issue because I'm heading to my office and your house is on the way.

No, Son, I don't want to trouble you.

No, Aunty, not at all.

Okay then.

I was following her instructions as we drove away.

Meanwhile, I told her she shouldn't worry her daughter since she may be studying only to hear what she had to say about Aadhya.

No Son! She works as a Software Engineer in a company near Nanakramguda.

Looking at you, I assumed you had a child who was still in school I said.

Haha. No Son.

What do you do? she asked.

I work as an HR manager for an MNC in Nanakramguda.

Ohh accha hei

Take the second left she said and I was both delighted and scared as I drove to her house. My heart was pounding, my palms were sweaty, and Aadhya was on her way to the hospital.

She stared at us and started ranting at her mother as soon as we arrived.

Mom! I told you I'd come. Why did you ask him to drive you home? You couldn't wait? she yelled.

No, Aadhya ji. I told her I'd drive her home because she had to wait there alone..

She glared at me and raged at her mother for revealing her identity to me.

No, I stepped in. I was taking back the phone from your mothert and while closing the app, I noticed the truecaller notification, and that's how I know your name I explained.

She ordered her mother to follow her inside, and she stormed in without saying a word.

I felt terrible about what had happened and was ready to start my bike to ride away when Aadhya stopped me,

"Hello, Excuse me!"

Yes!

Please do not take the initiative and become a hero the next time. We are conscious of our responsibilities and do not need help from others. What if I went to the hospital and didn't see my mother?
Please do not do this to anybody else. She stormed back inside again without letting me utter a single word.

What had happened had devastated me. But it was my fault for not informing her the situation, and she has every right to be upset, but I didn't anticipate our first meeting to be so tense. I started my bike and rode to work, saddened by what had happened.

The same evening..

My phone started ringing, and I saw it was Aadhya calling

in. My hands couldn't grasp my phone as it slipped away until I smacked so many things on the way to finally grab it and answer.

AB: Hello! Aadhya ji

AA: How do you know that it's me?

AB: As I told you in the morning, Truecaller!

AA: Ya, Whatever. Stop by our house once on your way back to home.

AB: Why ji?

AA: Bina bole nai aata kya?

AB: No no, just asking. I will I will

AA: Ha okay. Bye.

What just happened?

I was stunned and also was concerned because I was unaware of the consequences. I drove to her house and called her to let her know I had arrived.

She came downstairs, and I realised she was hiding something behind her back as she approached towards me, and I was waiting for the suspense to end.
She brought it in, and it was a lovely rose. She handed it to me and apologised and thanked me.

Why? I inquired.

I spoke with my mother after you left, and she informed me of what had happened. How she passed out, how you helped her, and how you cared for her. She also stated that you took her to a restaurant before dropping her off so that she would be comfortable during the ride. After listening to all that, I felt bad for talking to you in that way, and I couldn't just apologise over the phone or by text, so I asked you to come over. I sincerely regret what I said. I am sorry.

It's okay. Thanks for the rose.

Let me introduce myself, I'm Aadhya, she said as she extended her hand.

I'm Abhi, Abhiram and we shook hands.

Despite the fact that we both knew each other's names, this meeting and the handshake felt amazing.

All right, Aadhya ji. I'll leave now. Take care.

Thanks a lot Abhiram ji and I am really sorry. Byee

It's okay ji. Byee.

I began riding my bike away while glancing at her in the mirror as she walked back into the house until she vanished.

I touched her hand, it felt like I was touching an angel. It was unreal, and I was overtaken with delight and went straight to bed thinking about what had happened.

• • •

The following day...

I have her phone number, but I'm not sure how to approach her or what to ask. What if she thinks I'm insane?

While Brain was playing Q&A, time passed and I started preparing to leave for the office.

I got on my bike, but all I wanted to do was ride down her street and hope to see her.

Yayy!!

I noticed her standing outside her house, as usual, attempting to start her scooter.

I approached and said hello!

Hello. Who's this?

"Abhi!" I exclaimed while taking off my helmet.

Oh!
What are you doing here?

I was trying to avoid traffic when I found myself in your lane.
What happened to your bike, by the way? I inquired.

I don't know, she said with a sour tone.

I'm happy to drop you off at your office, I said.

No, it's fine. I'll take a cab. You must be on your way somewhere else, she said.

No! Aunty told me that you work in a company near Nanakramguda, and my company is also in that area, so it won't be a problem.

I tried to explain and convince her to say yes for couple of minutes only to hear three words.

Are you sure?

Yes, I exclaimed.

She said, "Okay," and hopped on the bike.

I've never ridden my bike slower than 60 mph, but today it's not going faster than 40 since I want this ride to go as long as possible.

Her mother called while she was driving.
I overheard the conversation and realised she didn't eat anything and was upset about something.
I asked her to get off the bike near a tiffin centre so she could eat something.

"Did I ask you?", she yelled. Don't take advantage because I'm taking your ride to work. I'll take a taxi instead and she started walking away.

Aadhya ji!
I apologise for doing things on my own, but I overheard the conversation and understood that you didn't have anything. So, please eat, I urged.

Are you crazy or what?
No one ever understands how I feel and only wants me to adjust to what is going on around, she shouted.

As peopled started staring at us, I hopped on my bike and asked her to join me so that I could drop her off at her office as soon as possible.

What? She inquired.

Nothing! Please accept my apologies.

She sat on the bike and we continued the ride.

Did you eat anything? she asked.

No ji. I'm fine, I said.

Why? she asked.

No, I don't eat alone if I'm with a friend, I replied.

When did we become friends? she inquired.

We can now, I giggled.

I checked her reaction in the mirror, but she was engrossed in her own thoughts. I left her just to be neglected and

forgotten. Though it stung a little, I was worried about her. What happened, and why is she acting this way?
I've seen her smiling and speaking politely to janitors and nurses, and her grin was an assurance to everyone that everything would be fine but now all I can see is her other side, which is not good since I know something is wrong.

I returned to my office but was only thinking about her.

It was almost lunchtime, and I was sitting at my desk trying to solve the puzzle when I received a text.

"AA: I'm sorry, Abhiram ji; I didn't intend to do what I did today, but there are few things I can't discuss with anybody, and we just met, and I know you're not like other people, but I'm someone who won't trust till I know them completely. I appreciate what you did that day, but I cannot accept you as a friend right now; I hope you understand.".

AB: It's okay Aadhya ji. I can understand. I am sorry too as I shouldn't have proceeded that quickly.

AA: It's okay. Had anything to eat?

AB: No. Wbu?

AA: I will and I am sorry. Please aap kuch khalo

AB: Yes yes I will and please you too eat something

AA: Yeah I will

AB: I can drop you off at home in the evening

AA: No. My company provides cabs in these cases and I already booked one.

AB: Okay.

AA: Thanks though!

AB: Not a problem, but would be my pleasure.

AA: Haha, still a no.

AB: Okay.

And the chat went on; at first, the topics were strictly business, but as the days passed, I learned more and more about her.

She is a South Mumbai girl who likes sitting on Marine Drive and eating vada pav while admiring nature's beauty. She was small and adorable, but most importantly, she was a brainy beauty.

We enjoyed each other's company, and the minutes turned into hours, days turned into weeks, and a month passed before I realised what was going on.

CHAPTER III

Asking out for a date

Sep 6, 2019

Despite the fact that we were frequently in touch, I never spent time with her or interacted with her outside of virtual texts. That was something I absolutely wanted to do. Though I asked her out on a date through text and erased it before she read it since I realised it was a poor idea. But this time I was determined, so I mustered all my bravery and eventually texted her.

AB: Hey, Wassup!!

AA: Nothing much. Bolo.

AB: Can I ask you something??

AA: Yeah..

AB: It's been almost a month and I'm thinking about us meeting someday to have lunch and all.

AA: Cool! We can do that. I will ask my friend to join.

AB: No no no

AA: Why?

AB: I meant, just two of us

AA: Ummm. Are you asking me to go on a date?

AB: No no no I mean yes but no not the date you are thinking but yes a friendly date. Just us I meant we both are good friends and I wanted to know about you more in person...

AA: Aha..
Okay
Cool
I'm in.

AB: Wow! Great!

AA: Haha

AB: Is Sunday fine? And evening 6PM?

AA: Yes, that will work.

AB: Great!! I will come pick you up.

AA: But, one condition

AB: What?

AA: It should not be any fancy restaurant because I don't like those places. Let's go to a place which has good food and not good bill

AB: Lol. Okay madam

AA: Whatelse?

....

And the chat went on until we both realised it was past midnight and we were both exhausted.

It was Saturday, and I had woken up early to plan how I could make it memorable. I've always wanted to take her out on a date, and the moment has finally arrived. I'll be with her. The whole idea was amazing and I couldn't believe what happened last night and continued reviewing the conversation to ensure it wasn't a dream.
I finally started putting my mind to work, just thinking about what to dress, where to g., and what vehicle to use. I only have a bike and must now get a car either for lease. My mind was racing with so many ideas that I instantly dialled Anil's number, who is an expert in all of them.

AB: Hey bro, I need your help.

AN: Bolo bhai.

AB: I need a car on Sunday from 5PM to 12AM.

AN: Hein? Why?

AB: I did, in fact, ask her out.

AN: What?

AB: Yes, I asked Aadhya out on a date on Sunday, I can't just show up on my bike, so please help me.

AN: Got you bhai. I'll call you in a while. You chill.

I kept thinking about the areas, and Anil phoned back within 10 minutes.

AN: Bhai, car sorted. I took care of everything and you will have it by tomorrow 5PM.

AB: Wow, Thanks bro.

One matter has been resolved. What else am I supposed to do now? I scribbled down every idea I had in my thoughts.

> Blue jeans, a blazer, white T-shirt, and white trainers
> Car
> Good restaurant - reserved a table
> Flowers - purchased and will be ready for tomorrow

Sorted..

I was delighted with the outcome, so I left everything aside and waited for the sun to rise. It wasn't a regular night. I heard the clock hit 12:00 and realised I'd have to wait another 18 hours more to see her.

Why!!!!!!

I've never been so irritated or impatient and I started chastisising the sun, moon, clock. Despite the fact that I couldn't wait, I enjoyed the feeling of waiting.

CHAPTER IV

Date Night

Sep 8, 2019

I used to look forward to waking up every morning to see what the world had in store for me. But this time it's different. I'm going to see the girl I'm crazy about. I planned on spending some time with her. After thinking all of that, I began to freshen up and was ready to go out, but it was still 11:00 a.m. What the hell happened to our clock? I yelled.

What happened? Why are you shouting? Mom inquired.

Nothing, I said. I walked into my room and locked the door, just to chuckle at myself for being so impatient and tried to relax.

After a while, I informed Mom that I had an official meeting and that I have to wear this Blazer and everything. Okay, she responded. I was getting ready to go. But it's 4 p.m. and I still haven't heard from Anil regarding the car.

I realised I needed to pull out the Blazer, only to find it missing from the closet. Where is my blazer? I yelled.

What happened? Mom inquired.

MOM!! Where's my Blazer???

How will I know? She replied.

Mom, please. Where is it?

I really don't know Abhi.

I searched everywhere, only to discover it drying in the sun, and it was all my maid's fault.

Aunty!!!!!
Why did you do that?
Who told you to wash it? What's the matter with you?

Abhi!! Put a stop to it.
What's the matter with you? Mom stepped in.
What's the point of yelling at her?
You have a lot of other clothes, and you like them all, so why the fuss? Go and wear something else She yelled.

My maid, who is above the age of 40. I always treated her with respect. I felt awful for shouting at her, but there was nothing I could do, so I dressed in a black shirt, blue pants and white sneakers. Despite the fact that it was my go-to attire, I wasn't satisfied this time.
It was akmost 5 p.m. when I got a text from Aadhya.

AA: "I'm ready and will be waiting for you <3"

I was furious and called Anil to inquire about the car. Much to my surprise, the car broke down, and they are hoping to deliver another one by 7 PM. I hung up the phone and began to ponder. The only thing remaining on my list was flowers, so I started my bike and prayed during the ride that the flowers plan shouldn't go wrong.

I travelled all the way, picked up the flowers I had ordered, and went to her house with disappointment since I wasn't feeling well and also because I was riding a bike rather than a car.

I arrived at her house and dialled her number.

She walked out with a long black gown, black heels, and a handbag in her hand. She wore her hair free to let it blow in the breeze. Her beauty took my breath away.

I couldn't move because I was taken aback by how beautiful she was.

As she caressed my shoulder, she said, "Abhi." That was a new experience and emotion for me. With butterflies in my stomach, I said, "Hi, you're looking gorgeous."

She smiled and replied, "Thank you." So....

I'm really sorry. Let's go, and please accept my heartfelt apologies. I had a lot of plans, but life had other ideas.

It's okay, Abhi. Getting on your bike is also nothing new. An open ride over a closed box is my preference.

That boosted my confidence, and I answered, "Let's go."

Are those flowers for me? she asked.

I'm sorry. Yes, they are. I was only concerned about how

you would react, and I had forgotten about these. Please accept it princess, I said.

She giggled as she took them.

So, let's go, I said.

She smiled as she nodded her approval.

I extended my hand for her to sit on my bike. She gave me an unhappy expression, but then she broke out laughing, took my hand, and sat on the bike. We rode to my next destination.

It was a famous restaurant in Madhapur with a pleasant atmosphere. I inquired as to whether she liked it or not.

Surprisingly, she looked at me and said, "I remember saying that any place is fine and its food should be good, not the bill."

I laughed and replied, "Yes, I remember." But this place has fantastic food, and I urge you to try it.

Please.... I requested.

Okay, she said, as we headed in. I adjusted the chair so she could sit, and then I gave her so many alternatives, only to get the response, "I'd like to know your taste." So, order whatever you want and I'll give it a go.
With a great smile on my face, I started going through the menu and ordered two courses and beverages.

We already know each other from our hourly discussions and texting. But I couldn't ask her anything because I was simply staring into her eyes and falling in love with her over and over again. Despite how regularly we communicated, I never questioned about her relationship status. I eventually worked up the guts to ask her and said, "I have a question for you." May I?

She nodded in approval.

I just want to know if you have... and pardon me, sir!!

The server brought us the meal we had ordered. Yes, please serve, and we started eating and cracking terrible jokes. It was ideal. But I'm still curious about what she thinks of me and if she has somebody significant in her life.

By the way, I never inquired about you, she said.

What? I asked.

It was always about me, your career, or our interests and gossips, but you never discussed your background, she said.

Oh!
I'm a South Indian who was born and raised in Hyderabad and I'm the only child.

Ohhhh!

Haha, Yes.

She asked me not to order any more food.

When we were done eating, I asked her, "How's the food and the place?"

Everything was okay, she replied.

Okay!!
So, what would be your ideal date? I asked.

She giggled and said, "All right, let's go."

Where? I inquired.

Chalo.. I started my bike as we rode towards Cyber Towers, and she asked me to pull over near the famous Madhapur street food line.

Why here? I asked.

You will see, she giggled.

Bhayya ek plate gulab jamun.

I was just staring at her and smiled. She fed me with her hands.

"The unexpected bite that landed in my mouth glazed with her hands will be my favorite memory for the rest of my life."

While I was still processing what had just occurred, Abhi! She exclaimed with delight, pointing to the adorable handbags with teddy bears. I saw her inner child emerge. I know she wants to purchase it, but she can't.

I'll get them for you, I said.

No, I don't like it when others buy things for me.

I'll get it later. Chalo!

While walking down the street she inquired as to whether or not I had a girlfriend.

No! I replied, "Not at all."

Oh! I was hoping for one, she said.

What made you believe it? I inquired.

Nothing! And then she started walking away.

What about you? I asked. Do you have anyone special in your life?

Yes, she said, and my heart skipped a beat.

Okay, great, I said as my head went blank and I felt like I'd been hit by a truck.

After a minute of stillness, she chuckled and replied, "No, I don't have a boyfriend, but I do believe I have a special person, a good friend, and I am now walking only with him."

I was unsure for a while, realising what she had said, and I became overwhelmed with emotions.

"Oh no, it's already 9 o'clock," she exclaimed. My dad will be home by 10 o'clock." I had to get home before he arrives.

I told her to leave it to me. I started my bike and we arrived in KPHB in 15 minutes. I dropped her off. We exchanged handshakes and I just watched her walk to her house. We exchanged handshakes, and I just stood there watching her walk to her house. She abruptly turned around and returned for a hug. She slipped away before I could respond, and I couldn't see her again. I grinned, only to realise I hadn't awoken from a nightmare. I began riding my bike back home.

Despite the fact that I had already visited the location. Everything now reminds me of her. The routes, places, and even my bike appeared to be new. How strange the day began and how beautifully it ended. I suddenly felt like the luckiest guy in the whole wide world.

When I got home, I saw her SMS asking if I was okay. It's a lovely feeling to receive a text from someone who cares about how you're doing and where you're going, and I just said yes.

"I was having a difficult time and didn't know what to do. Today, on the other hand, is one of those days that I will never forget. Thank you very much, Abhi. <3
Now it's time to call it a night. Good night, Sweet dreams, Take care", she texted.

Thank you for taking the time to consider my request and

for giving me such beautiful memories. Thank you, Aadhya.
Good night. I replied.

CHAPTER V

Falling in love

Oct 15, 2019

The intended day trips became unanticipated night rides. It was a lovely feeling, but I'm still unsure what we are for one other. We never talked about how we felt. But we're having fun with one other and enjoying every minute that life has to offer.

I went to the workplace to pick her up. She texted her father, that she would be late due to extra work and would arrive home at 2 AM.
I enjoyed how she lied to their family so she could spend more time with me. I inquired where she wanted me to take her.

DLF? She uttered

Haha Let's go, madam, I said.

We drove to the location. In the renowned AM-PM, she ordered some fries and her favourite hazelnut cold coffee.

I was admiring her eyes, attractiveness, and the way she was chowing down on the food she had ordered while having fun with it. It gave me the impression that I was seeing a rabbit eat carrots.

She inquired as to what had caused my giggle. Nothing I

said.

Bolo na! she demanded.

You remind me of an adorable rabbit chewing a carrot, I said, laughing.

Abhi!!!! Stop it!!
"I'll kill you," she muttered as she tapped my shoulder.."

A voice echoed from behind, "Kill me, darling."

I turned around to find a drunk and his pal, neither of whom seemed conscious of their surroundings.

We made an attempt to ignore them and continued on our way. They followed and began chattering.

Do you want me to show how to love her? he asked.
And he started moving forward.

What are you thinking, you moron? I yelled.

Brother, please relax. I feel she is dissatisfied with you, and I will show you how to love her.

I grabbed his collar and starting pounding him. Finally got both drunks to collapse, and then began kicking both of them.

Abhi!!!
Aadhya shouted, terrified of what would happen to me if something happened to them.

She urged everyone to leave. She seized my hand and began trying to pull me away from those imbeciles.

What?? I gave her an angry-looking stare.

She gave me a startled look as she started crying and pleaded for us to leave.

I don't want this at all. Let's go, please, she begged.

I calmed myself as I looked at her tears and held her, saying, "I'm sorry, Aadhya." Once again, I apologise and asked her to take a look at me.

That was the first time I saw her weep, as she turned to face me, afraid and with red eyes.

I genuinely want to kill those idiots, but we're leaving. Let's get going, I said as we started walking away from them without looking back.

We hopped on my bike and drove off.

I asked her if she was okay and apologised for what had happened.

No, Abhi. But, why you behaved the way you did. We could have just left, but you got into a fight with him. Why? she inquired.

I don't know Aadhya. I like you, I'll be honest. Not even like, "I love you".

I Love You, Aadhya.

Since the first moment I saw you, I've had the impression you're the person I need in my life. Why, you could ask? I'm not sure what my reaction would be. I stated this as I looked at her in the mirror. I love you, Aadhya. I swear to look out for you and treat you with dignity. I will never cause you harm. I'd even like to marry you. But just don't leave me as a friend.

Abhi! Stop the bike! she exclaimed.

Why Aadhya? What happened? I inquired as my heartbeat raced.

Stop it now! she ordered.

Okay. And we came to a halt.

What happened, Aadhya? I inquired.
I'm truly sorry. I really shouldn't have said it. I apologise, I said.

Be quiet, Abhi, she said as there was a one-minute stillness.

I was terrified as she might decide to cease being my friend. Why did I tell her now? I simply wish I could go back in time and change everything.

Abhi, I have some questions, she said.

Yes, Aadhya. What are they? I inquired.

Do you genuinely care for me? she asked.

Yes, Aadhya, and as I said...

Shushh.. Just reply "yes" or "no"?

Yes, I replied.

Even if it exceeds your budget, will you still buy me whatever I ask for? she asked.

Yes, I replied.

And lastly, will you safeguard me the same way you did tonight? she asked.

Yes, even if it means losing my life, Aadhya.

I was smacked and questioned, "Did I ask for that?"
Just don't say that to me again, she uttered.

I love you, Abhi, and I don't want anything, she whispered as she wrapped her arms around me as her eyes welled up with tears. I don't need anything. I want your love, protection, and care.
I am sorry for smacking you. I love you, you moron!

I was stunned to realise what had just occurred as I felt the warmth of the hug. It was impossible for me to believe that she was now mine and that we were dating since I had never seen somebody as gorgeous and kind as she was.
She's in my arms, and I want to hold her there until I die.

When we were engrossed in our own world, A bunch of people suddenly sped by us, shouting "Love birds".

We laughed as soon as we realised we were still on the road and got on my bike to go to Aadhya's house to drop her off.

Abhi, wait, she said as she turned back.

What happened? I asked.

Nothing! She nodded, hugged me, and kissed me on the cheek before rushing back to her house.

I was stunned and tried to make sense of all that happened.

I once more glanced at her house, but I was unable to see her. With a large smile on my face and a heart full of happiness, I hopped on my bike to ride back home, as I was just thinking about everything that had happened—it is still unbelievable.

CHAPTER VI

Unexpected Trip

Oct 28, 2019

I was about to go for work when I got a phone call from Aadhya.

AB: Hi Aadhya! Good morning!

AA: Hey Abhi.

AB: What prompted madam to call me at this time?

AA: I'm actually going on a trip and thought I'd invite you along.

AB: Of Course I would love to! But, when and where?

AA: Today!

AB: What? You are joking right?

AA: No. Today. Will you be able to make it or not?

AB: Yes Yes Of Course I will.

AA: Come to MGBS at 4:30PM today.

AB: But where are we going?

AA: Will tell you later. Don't be late.

AB: Sure will be there. Bye my love!

AA: Haha bye Idiot!

A trip with Aadhya. I was as delighted about going on vacation as a youngster. What to say at home and at work was the first thing that sprang to mind. Worse, I have no clue how long the trip will take.
Let it be! First, I'll take a sick leave, and then I'll be able to manage in the office. I soon submitted a sick leave request to the management, which was also accepted.

Mom! I yelled in excitement.

What Abhi? she inquired.

I'm going to work at a friend's house and will be there for several days since we have a lot of work.

Okay Abhi, she replied.

Please tell Dad too, I said.

Okay, you go, she said.

Everyone and everything seemed to want me to go on this vacation.

I was overjoyed and began packing. I was unsure about the location, so I packed a couple of jeans, t-shirts, and a sweater because it was winter.

I reached MGBS and dialled her number.

Hey Abhi! Come to platform number 45 she said.

Okay, I said as I started heading towards the platform, where I spotted her standing with a tall and fair guy. Aadhya signalled for me to behave normally as I approached since I was going to offer her a hug.
For a few seconds, I couldn't understand until she offered me a handshake and said, "Hey Abhi." This is Ayaan, my brother and Ayaan, he is Abhi, my friend.

Friend! I was confused.
Okay, she must not have told him about our relationship, and that's OK; I approached him to offer him a handshake, only to have him ignore me and tell me that it's becoming late and we need to board the bus.

By the way, where are we going, I asked.

Her brother began to look sceptical, and Aadhya intervened, saying, Lol Abhi, You'd been wanting to go to Tirupati for a long time, and we'd wanted to go as well. Now that we can, we thought we'd go together, na, because you know the place better than we do.

I was stunned, but I managed to say Yes, you are correct.

I was joking, Let's go, I said.

They both sat in the front seats, leaving me in the back. I was really curious about what's going on. I tried calling her, but she didn't answer and didn't respond to my messages.

Our journey began, and we continued to travel through various areas. The bus eventually came to a stop for a dinner break, and we three exited to get food and eat. I couldn't talk to her as I used to because of her brother. Finally, he walked to the loo, leaving us two alone, and I started questioning her.

Aadhya What exactly is going on?
You just mentioned a trip but didn't mention your brother, and we're going to Tirupati?
What's all this? I asked.

Calm down, Abhi.
I realise I made a mistake, but I really wanted to go to Tirupati with you, and I figured you'd go anyplace with me, but you're upset with the location. I didn't anticipate this from you, and my brother was not in the plan, but I failed to convince my parents otherwise, so here we are. I won't push you to come with me or anything, Abhi, but it's entirely up to you, she said saddenedly.

I apologise and understand, Aadhya. It had nothing to do with location. I just imagined a vacation meant we were going somewhere to spend time together, and I had no idea Mumbai locals were familiar with Tirupati.

Of course we do. What do you think of us? she questioned.

No, I didn't mean that, and we laughed until he arrived and began asking her sister to finish quickly and board the bus to sleep.

Dude! Why are you so hurried? Allow her to eat gently, and Bus will not start right away.

See bro! It's none of your business, and he began walking her back to the bus.

I know he's her brother, but I didn't like the way he controls her sister. I, too, boarded the bus while looking at her sorry face and dozed off.

• • •

Oct 29, 2019

We arrived at Tirupati bus depot around 5 AM and I got down to go get the bus tickets for Tirumala and asked them to get ready.

No, she stopped me and said, "We'll take the steps."

What? We were both surprised as we'd never expected this from her, and for the first time, we both were on the same page.

My brain finished all the calculation, and I began explaining why we were saying no to her. Aadhya, there are over two thousand steps in one and over three thousand steps in the other, and this is your first time, so we don't want you to do this.

Shut up, girls, I know what I'm doing and I'm going to take

Srivari mettu steps, she said.

Though her brother and I tried desperately to convince her, we were unsuccessful and took an auto rickshaw to Srivari mettu after getting ready.

I asked her again just to make sure she really wanted to do it.

She said yes, so we left our luggage in the luggage room and began climbing the stairs.

We were taking breaks because her brother and I were struggling, but we had to stop Aadhya in between to take a break, and after an hour, we finished climbing the stairs and reached Tirumala.

It was a beautiful sight, and as a Telugu guy, I had always wanted to visit Tirupati with my soulmate, and as I looked at her, I smiled brightly because it had come true even before I imagined it.

We reserved a room to freshen up. We returned only to find Aadhya dressed in a red saree with loose hair. I stopped breathing for a second because I was so taken with her beauty that I couldn't believe what I was seeing.

Ayaan said, "Bro, let's go." But I was only thinking about my princess as she approached.

He snapped his fingers, bro. Yes, Yes, I replied, and looking at her, I went in to get dressed, and we began walking towards the entry gate.

It was a weekday, but the crowd made it feel like a Sunday. Over 50K people had already gathered.
We entered the gate and began walking in the queue, and after an hour of walking, we arrived at the waiting halls, where I explained everything to them both and felt like I was a guide for them on this trip.

After 30 minutes of waiting, we went inside the main gopuram only to see Balaji for 2 seconds.

I asked how she was after darshan, and she was overjoyed, and gave me a bear hug, oblivious to the fact that her brother was standing next to us. I didn't say much except that her brother was watching us.

She got it and said, "Let's go now."

We returned to our rooms after taking Laddoos to Tirupati from Tirumala.

Ayaan began staring at us strangely the moment she hugged me, but I ignored him and his stares as I asked Aadhya where she wanted to go next. She said she didn't know because she just wanted to sleep for the night.

We then went on to look for a good hotel to stay at and ended up booking two rooms, one for them and one for me.

Aadhya texted that Ayaan had gone out to bring food and she wanted to speak with me personally. So I went into her room and saw her crying as her brother began asking her questions about us.

Aadhya Nothing will happen. I'll make sure everything falls in it's place.

What if my parents don't agree?

I will convince them. We will wait and fight for ourselves until they see how much we love each other.

I don't know Abhi. I just want you and to live with you until the end of my life; I don't want to die.

Die? Are you crazy, Aadhya?

Do not say such things, please. I hugged her and cried with her. Looking at her was causing me pain. Her soft cheeks deserve a smile, not tears. I kissed her on the forehead and wiped her tears away, assuring her that nothing bad would happen to us and that we would be together forever.

Her brother arrived unexpectedly, only to see us both hugging.

He rushed in only to separate us and yell at her sister.

What's the matter with you? Have you thought what will happen to Mom and Dad if they get to know all this? he yelled.

I asked Ayaan to please calm down.

You don't come between us, you jerk; what have you done to her? he yelled.

"Get out of this room!" he yelled.

Ayaan, we're not teenagers, we know what we're doing, and we're thinking about meeting your parents after this.

"Dude, you don't understand, first get out!" he yelled.

Aadhya was crying, and even though he is her brother, I couldn't leave her alone with him.

I moved forward to comfort her, but Ayaan grabbed my collar and tried to threw me out, and I raised my hand only to see Aadhya in the background pleading that I return to my room and stop this here.

After a while, I texted her to see how she was doing, but she didn't respond. When I called her, her phone was turned off.

I sat in my room, thinking about her. I waited until morning before knocking on their door. There was no response, soon the hotel staff member arrived with keys to open and clean the room. I asked him where everyone in this room was. He said he didn't know and directed me to reception.

I dashed downstairs to see what had happened and discovered that they had checked out and had immediately booked a cab from the hotel to the bus depot.

There was no message, phone call, or hint.

I was devastated, but I accepted what had happened and

returned to the bus depot to return to Hyderabad.

The trip, which began unexpectedly, ended unexpectedly in a strange turn of events.

All I could think about was Aadhya.

How is she doing? Is she all right? Did Ayaan reveal everything in her home?
Why isn't she texting or calling me?

I couldn't close my eyes or think about anything but Aadhya. I attempted to call her several times but was unsuccessful. I contacted her friends, but no one knows where she is or what she is dealing with.

When I finally arrived in Hyderabad, the first thing I wanted to do was go to her house and see how she was.

I went to my friend's house to get my bike and started riding towards her house. When I arrived at her home, it was locked. I even asked her neighbors, and all they said was, "We don't know."

I tried calling her repeatedly, but her phone was turned off. I tried every social media platform but was unsuccessful.

Everything seemed to be coming to an end, but I had no idea what was going on.

After a while, I got a call from one of her friends saying that Aadhya doesn't want you to see her again, that she can't disobey her parents, and that she has to marry someone else whom they had set up for her a long time ago. She also asked you not to look for her anywhere.

Are you serious? Where is she now? I yelled.

I don't know Abhi, and the phone call was disconnected.

I stumbled down as I tried to process everything that had just happened as it felt like the ground beneath me was broken.
The girl I believed would be mine is no longer mine. She simply accepted her faith without telling me about her problems. We were together, and she never told me about her getting married to someone else.

I couldn't stop crying, and I couldn't stop hurting myself physically and emotionally to figure out what was going on.

I was going insane.

Why should you accept my love in the first place?

Why should you give me hope?

I thought true love existed, but it does not. It's all rubbish.

But, should I believe her friend?

What if everything she said is true? What if it isn't?

So many questions popped up, only to aggravate me.

Days passed, but my feelings for her did not. I couldn't speak to her or see her one more time. All I was thinking was to drink and forget what had happened, or death.

46

CHAPTER VII

I.C.U

Dec 11, 2019

My phone started ringing. As I looked at it, it showed a landline number from a hospital. I didn't think it was important, but I decided to respond anyway. I recognised a familiar voice, and it was her friend Archana. She was sobbing so hard I could hardly make out anything that she was blabbering. In between the broken sobs she gave me the name of the hospital and asked me to reach there ASAP. Nothing made any sense to me. I asked her what was wrong. In one breath she uttered "Aadhya,".
My world spinned so fast, I couldn't understand anything but her name turned my eyes moist and my heart beat paced. I was filled with a million thoughts, I wasn't aware till I heard my own sound vibrating through the room "What happened to her?" Is she alright?

Please come to this hospital right away in KPHB, she said.

I told my parents I had to leave and would be late and dashed out the door, forgetting to take the bike keys. I went back to fetch the keys and fell down the stairs, bruising myself on the way, but I didn't really care as she was the only one on my mind at that moment.

Despite being just a 2-kilometer drive, it appeared to take forever. When I got to the hospital, I asked the receptionist for the room number.

I.C.U., she said.

"I.C.U," I hollered.

I was at a loss for words. I sprinted like a lunatic, my eyes searching for that one person who holds my heart.

As soon as I arrived at the I.C.U. ward, my lips began to quiver and started a silent prayer on their own. I saw Aadhya's mom, dad, and brother standing and crying, watching someone in the intensive care unit. I saw my friends along with hers. I stood there dumbstruck, unable to move when someone grabbed my wrist. It was Ayaan, her brother. He had pleaded with me to go inside and talk to Aadhya.

Aadhya was in the I.C.U. with all the wires attached, I could see her heartbeat on the screen, yet my eyes refused to believe what they saw. I can't even feel the ground beneath me. My feet were numb and my palms ice cold. My world had already crumbled with that one phone call.

I was startled to hear when a voice ask, "Are you Mr. Abhiram?"

With tears in my eyes, I said yes to the nurse while my eyes still glued to Aadhya.

Please don't take too long, she needs to rest. The nurse exited the room, leaving the two of us alone.

I sat beside her bed, taking her hand in mine. She was

lying still surrounded by all the tubes and wires yet nothing could take away the beauty that she held. Even in that stillness, she was the most beautiful, most precious person to me on this earth.

I knew she couldn't hear me but I had to try. That's my girl right there.

I went near her ear and whispered softly.*Aadhya..

"Abhi....," echoed a voice.

When I saw Aadhya, she stared at me with tears in her eyes. Did you come to visit me? She was perplexed.

Why would I not? I was only waiting for your phone call. But, what is this all about? What's going on? Why are you here? What happened to you? I asked in agony.

Abhi, I'm going to die, she answered.

"Die!!"

What!!!!

It's not true. Don't talk like that, or I'll kill you, I yelled.

But it's true, Abhi. Myeloma is a rare blood cancer. And there is no cure. I don't have much time, Abhi, and all I want right now is to die in your hands.

No!! Stop It!!

You are not going to die.

Doctor!!!

I shouted in anguish and started to walk out of the room. Aadhya took my hand in hers, motioned for me to sit. "I want you to be with me for the last minutes of my life", she said.

"I don't want to leave you without telling you because I want you to be happy, so promise me you'll smile whenever you think of me." That is the only thing I want from you."

Please, Aadhya, don't say that. I cried out, "You're not going to die."

Abhi, I still remember the first time I saw you. You were sitting next to your father, staring at me....

and she became unconscious.

What happened, Aadhya?

Aadhya!!!

Wake up, Comeon!

Aadhya!!!

I stroked her hands. Patted her cheeks.

Nothing will happen to you; I will save you. Please don't

leave me, I cried.

She regained consciousness and said Abhi..
I'm quite sure I'm not going to make it. I can feel it. Please promise me that you will never cry over me and that you will go on to achieve great things in your life.
Please make a promise to me.

Please, Aadhya. Don't say anything like that. You will not die. I sobbed.

Abhi... and she passed out again.

Aadhya! Aadhya! I yelled, "Wake up!"

Nurse entered the room and requested me to go, but I couldn't since I wanted to be with her, but they asked her family to leave, so I had to leave while refusing their request.

Doctor inquired about Abhiram and requested that her family accompany me inside as she is conscious.

I dashed in only to find that her heart rate was rapidly declining and she wanted me to hold her hand and look at her. While her parents were sobbing, the only words that came out of her mouth were,

"Mom, Dad, Brother, Abhi - I love you all."
Thank you for everything, and Abhi, I am really sorry for leaving you so soon, but I will see you from heaven, and I want you to look at the sky because that is where I will be.

I beg you, Aadhya, Please don't say that. You can't do this

to me. Please don't leave me, I cried.

Abhi...

I looked at her, and she was gone to rest among the stars while leaving me alone in the darkness.

Doctor Please do something, I yelled. Please

She's just passed out once more and she will regain conscious, I know that. Please do something, I screamed.

Please...

Abhi, she's gone, Ayaan tried to make me accept it.

No, don't say that; I'll kill you all. She promised to be there with me till my last breath.

As I tried to wake her up the only words I hear were she's gone, sir. We are completely helpless. Please accept it.

No, she's faking it, I know and I ran out heading straight to the parking lot.

Where are you going, Abhi? Stop!! Anil yelled and followed me until I fell off and hit a pillar.

I got up and started heading towards my bike. Anil came up behind me and began pulling me away from the bike. Are you an idiot? he yelled.

Please leave me alone. I have to go to Aadhya's favorite spot.

She'll come looking for me. I know.

Abhi, Aadhya left us, and you must accept this. Please try to understand.

He escorted me back upstairs, where I spotted my white-dressed angel, and we led her back to her home.

Relatives gathered and began preparing to carry her corpse to Mumbai, where she was born.

I requested if I might come, and with their approval, I went to Mumbai to see my angel one final time.

• • •

Dec 12, 2019

When we landed in Mumbai, her whole family was there, waiting for us to take one final look. I'd never forget that place. People were sobbing, passing out, and obsessing over her. My angel showed how to live good and be there for people even when things were not going well. We brought her to the funeral home. I couldn't see her in the fire, and I resisted stepping in because I wanted to remember her face, not the recollection of seeing her in flames.

Abhi! Beta! Aadhya's mother called, crying.

Son, this is Aadhya's diary.
She handed it to me when she was in the hospital and told me to give it to my love.

I took the diary from her and It's a lovely diary with flowers and a heart on it. I said farewell to everyone before continuing on with what had transpired so swiftly.

54

CHAPTER VIII

The Diary: My life changer

Dec 12, 2019 at 4PM

I went to Marine Drive (My angel's favorite spot) to see what she had left for me.

July 9, 2019
I saw him for the first time in the hospital. He was around 6 feet tall, cute, and appealing. It's the same as falling in love at first sight. But I observed how he looked at me and assumed he felt the same way.
I was so happy that I hurt my cheeks with my smile.

I sat in front of him despite the fact that there were so many empty seats. He was in the company of his father. I can sense he's excited to talk to me. The nurse called his father, and they entered. I had to see my doctor at the same time, and I was afraid we'd never see each other again. I searched for him but couldn't find him.

After 5 days, I had to return to the hospital for the test results and to meet the doctor, but he was not present as planned. I turned around and saw him conversing with the security guard about the parking problem, but he was nice to the guards, which I loved. My mother began to cry for no apparent reason, and I attempted to console her only to notice that he was sitting across from me.

Aadhya! When the nurse called my name, I was expecting him to hear it, but I was also frightened since I didn't want him to know I was the patient. The nurse, however, saved me by asking to take my mother inside.

While I was waiting in the corridor, a man from the medical store approached me and asked me to give the card to someone who had misplaced it. When I looked at the card for the name, it said "Abhiram."
I called Abhiram, and to my surprise, it 's him, the man I had fallen in love with. I liked how shy he was while accepting the card and I really wanted him to speak something.

As he left the place, I went back in only to find out that my mother was crying and when I was called back in. I sat down, and the doctor informed me that I have Myeloma, a rare blood cancer, and that even though it can be diagnosed, I won't live more than 5-6 months because it's in terminal stage. I was vomiting blood and other things and assumed it was an infection, but it turned out to be cancer.

I was devastated because I had hoped for so much and wanted to accomplish so much, but life had other plans for me.

I was unable to express myself. I began yelling at people. I couldn't smile and had given up on everything.

I stopped going to the hospital for reports or medication because I don't want to see my love Abhi and the thought of not living forever with him was even more painful and eventually would break my heart.

Days passed, and one day I received a call from an unknown number, which appeared in truecaller as Abhiram. I remembered it was him and stutteringly replied, but it's my Mom. I told her to wait an hour and then disconnected because I didn't want to talk to him. But, after staring at his phone number for so long, I'm not sure if this Abhiram is the same.

After 30 minutes, I began to approach my scooty to go to the hospital, only to be surprised to see my mother getting off a bike and the driver removing his helmet.
It had to be Abhiram. I couldn't believe my eyes and also didn't want it because I didn't want to feel all of this.

I started yelling at her and rushed her inside because I knew what would happen if I talked to him.

Though I felt bad about it, I had no choice.

When I entered, my mother explained what had happened and why she needed someone's assistance. I felt terrible about my actions. I inquired as to whether or not the number belonged to him. When she said yes, I immediately saved his phone number as if it were a lottery ticket.

I liked what I'm feeling, but I don't want to because my conscious is constantly telling me about my situation.

I didn't want to be respectful to him. I wanted him to despise me so he wouldn't develop feelings for me.

He was, however, far too nice and sweet. Instead, he transformed me into his friend.
I never expected to become friends with someone so quickly, and all I was doing was texting him all hours of the day and night.

Though he never asked me out or asked me any personal questions, which was one of the things I liked best about him.

This feeling is one that I both like and detest.

The date was September 6, 2019, and I will never forget it.

We were texting when my idiot unexpectedly asked me out on a date. I was struggling inside by masking my emotions in order to appear calm in front of him.
I liked how he approached me.
I said yes, only to struggle internally about what to wear and so on.
The date was September 8, 2019.

He arrived wearing a black shirt and jeans that matched the colour of my outfit. He was manly and tall, but he was so cute when he just stared at me without saying anything.
I knew what was going on with him, so I tapped his shoulder, and he was lost. I was overjoyed that he arrived by bike because I wanted to be closer to him rather than in a car sitting apart.

He explained why he was riding his bike rather than driving, as a student would explain to a teacher.
He brought me flowers, yayy.
I was overjoyed.
He extended his hand so I could hold his hand while sitting on the bike, which gave me butterflies.
I tried to be as normal as possible throughout the entire drive.
As usual, the boys don't understand what we're saying, so they took me to a high-end restaurant where the food was expensive but not particularly tasty.

Idiot wanted to impress me, but I didn't want the date to end, so I asked him to take me to Madhapur street food so I could spend more time with him.

I understand how he feels about me, so I wanted to play with him. So I spoon-fed him a gulab jamun.
I'm not sure what's wrong with me. Haha

The time had come for him to drop me off at my house, and I couldn't leave him like that, so I gave him a hug.

He thought we were best friends now, but he has no idea that I have been in love with him since the first time I saw him, and my feelings for him are growing stronger by the day.

It was October 15, 2019, and it was my favorite day of my life.

He came over to pick me up from the office, and we agreed to meet at DLF.

While we were eating, some thugs began harassing me.

My prince kicked and beat them like anything, and while I was enjoying everything, I heard someone say call the cops, and I became concerned and asked him to stop, but he didn't. I was scared, so I drew him back, and that was the first time I saw him angry.

I was scared looking at him because I should have stopped it earlier, but he understood and we began driving away from that location.

I was curious as to why he did all of this, so I asked him.

He surprised me by confessing his feelings for me and talking about getting married.
I couldn't take it anymore and asked him to stop.

When he kept asking me what happened, I was fighting with myself.

I have to respond, but I don't want to tell him about my situation.

I then asked him some questions, to which he always said yes.

I felt like I was already late in telling him how I felt, so I said I love you too and hugged him so tightly that I can still feel his warm embrace, smell his fragrance, and hear his heartbeat.

Every day for 13 days, he treated me like a Queen. He is my king.

But my days were getting shorter when I noticed that my blood vomits started to increase.

I really want to go on a trip and tried to convince my parents. Even though they are aware of my feelings, they do not want me to travel alone due to my medical condition.

I couldn't tell Abhi everything, but I trusted my instincts that he'd be fine with what was going on.
Fortunately, he said yes.

I was concerned because my brother was upset with me for making a guy's life miserable because I wouldn't be there with

him and he didn't know about it.
But I'm at a loss for what to do.

My brother was acting strangely in front of him because he knew about Abhi because he was at home when Abhi dropped my mother off and has known about him since then. He expected me to be a good friend and tell him everything, but I kept it a secret, which irritated him.

I even took steps in Tirupati because I didn't know when my last day would be and I wanted to spend as much time as possible with Abhi.
I recall him staring at me when I was dressed in that red saree. It was actually purchased by Abhi, but he is unaware that I will be wearing it. That entire day, I admired the way he saw me.

After darshan, we went down to my room, where I vomited blood and felt dizzy. That is why Ayaan had to leave. But I wanted Abhi near me because I thought I was going to die, but instead I started talking to him about something else.

I recall Ayaan marching in and starting yelling at Abhi because Ayaan felt bad for Abhi and was angry at me.
I felt dizzy after what happened, and he had to drive me back to Hyderabad because he didn't want Abhi to be disturbed any further.

Abhi my love,

Yes, I know you're going to read this and I really want you to as I left you with so much pain and I really want you to know my side story of how much I loved you every second.

I am sorry.
I involved you in all of this.
I deeply regret giving you hope.
I sincerely apologise for everything that happened.

But I was always in love with you.
I became selfish in order to have your love, care and respect even though I know I will die soon, and I am sorry for that.

My body will be ash by the time you read this, and my soul will be glancing at you.

I will always be by your side. Please just look at the sky and talk to me. That is the only desire I have.

Please move on in life.

Goodbye, Idiot.
My king, My Love, My everything.
<3 <3 <3

As I wiped my tears, I saw Aadhya, bright and shine smiling at me as she faded away into the sky, while the sunset hues surrounding her, disappeared into the vast deep blue sea.

The sun will set and rise every day, the rays will touch each of us but not my angel.

My girl, my angel, is gone. Will there ever be light in my life again?

THE END

63

www.ingramcontent.com/pod-product-compliance
Lightning Source LLC
Chambersburg PA
CBHW020752160726
47993CB00006B/2725